This planner belongs to:

Copyright © 2024 by Annette Bridges

www.annettebridges.com

Published by Ranch House Press

All rights reserved. Except as permitted under the U.S. Copyright Act of 1976, no part of this publication may be reproduced, distributed, or transmitted in any form or by any means, or stored in a database or retrieval system, without the prior written permision of the author.

Snowbaby is a white blue-eyed feline that lives on a cattle ranch in Texas. Original photographs of Snowbaby were taken by Annette Bridges.

Designed and Illustrated by Janie Owen-Bugh
www.janieowenbugh.com

Printed in the United States of America.

ISBN: 978-1-946371-51-5

ABOUT
Snowbaby, the cat

The beautiful white feline with gorgeous blue eyes featured in this personal planner lives on a cattle ranch in Texas. She was once a feral kitten whose mamma deserted her in the tree where she was born. She still lives in her beloved tree that is now inside of a huge catio built especially for her.

She adopted a human mamma named Annette who is the publisher of this personal planner. Annette soon learned that karma really is a cat and the cat is named Snowbaby.

Notes

"Sweet like honey, karma is a cat purring in my lap 'cause it loves me."
— TAYLOR SWIFT

January 2025

SUNDAY	MONDAY	TUESDAY	WEDNESDAY	THURSDAY	FRIDAY	SATURDAY
			1 New Year's Day	2	3	4
5	6	7	8	9	10	11
12	13	14	15	16	17	18
19	20 Martin Luther King Day	21	22	23	24	25
26	27	28	29	30	31	

Notes

"A cat has absolute emotional honesty: human beings, for one reason or another may hide their feelings but a cat does not."
— ERNEST HEMINGWAY

February 2025

SUNDAY	MONDAY	TUESDAY	WEDNESDAY	THURSDAY	FRIDAY	SATURDAY
						1
2	3	4	5	6	7	8
9	10	11	12	13	14 Valentine's Day	15
16	17 Presidents Day	18	19	20	21	22
23	24	25	26	27	28	

Notes

"The smallest feline is a masterpiece."
— LEONARDO DA VINCI

March 2025

SUNDAY	MONDAY	TUESDAY	WEDNESDAY	THURSDAY	FRIDAY	SATURDAY
						1
2	3	4	5	6	7	8
9	10	11	12	13	14	15
16	17	18	19	20	21	22
23	24	25	26	27	28	29
30	31					

Notes

"What greater gift than the love of a cat."
— CHARLES DICKENS

April 2025

SUNDAY	MONDAY	TUESDAY	WEDNESDAY	THURSDAY	FRIDAY	SATURDAY
		1	2	3	4	5
6	7	8	9	10	11	12
13	14	15	16	17	18	19
20 Easter	21	22	23	24	25	26
27	28	29	30			

Notes

"In ancient times cats were worshipped as gods;
they have not forgotten this."
— TERRY PRATCHETT

May 2025

SUNDAY	MONDAY	TUESDAY	WEDNESDAY	THURSDAY	FRIDAY	SATURDAY
				1	2	3
4	5	6	7	8	9	10
11 Mother's Day	12	13	14	15	16	17
18	19	20	21	22	23	24
25	26 Memorial Day	27	28	29	30	31

Notes

"There are two means of refuge from the miseries of life: music and cats."
— ALBERT SCHWEITZER

June 2025

SUNDAY	MONDAY	TUESDAY	WEDNESDAY	THURSDAY	FRIDAY	SATURDAY
1	2	3	4	5	6	7
8	9	10	11	12	13	14
15 Father's Day	16	17	18	19 Juneteenth	20	21
22	23	24	25	26	27	28
29	30					

Notes

"A meow massages the heart."
— STUART MCMILLAN

July 2025

SUNDAY	MONDAY	TUESDAY	WEDNESDAY	THURSDAY	FRIDAY	SATURDAY
		1	2	3	4 Independence Day	5
6	7	8	9	10	11	12
13	14	15	16	17	18	19
20	21	22	23	24	25	26
27	28	29	30	31		

Notes

"Meow means woof in cat."
— GEORGE CARLIN

August 2025

SUNDAY	MONDAY	TUESDAY	WEDNESDAY	THURSDAY	FRIDAY	SATURDAY
					1	2
3	4	5	6	7	8	9
10	11	12	13	14	15	16
17	18	19	20	21	22	23
24	25	26	27	28	29	30
31						

Notes

> "I have lived with several Zen masters — all of them cats."
> — ECKHART TOLLE

September 2025

SUNDAY	MONDAY	TUESDAY	WEDNESDAY	THURSDAY	FRIDAY	SATURDAY
	1 Labor Day	2	3	4	5	6
7	8	9	10	11	12	13
14	15	16	17	18	19	20
21	22	23	24	25	26	27
28	29	30				

Notes

"My dear, I'm a cat. Everything I see is mine."
— RICK RIORDAN

October 2025

SUNDAY	MONDAY	TUESDAY	WEDNESDAY	THURSDAY	FRIDAY	SATURDAY
			1	2	3	4
5	6	7	8	9	10	11
12	13 Columbus Day	14	15	16	17	18
19	20	21	22	23	24	25
26	27	28	29	30	31 Halloween	

Notes

"Never try to outstubborn a cat."
— ROBERT HEINLEIN

November 2025

SUNDAY	MONDAY	TUESDAY	WEDNESDAY	THURSDAY	FRIDAY	SATURDAY
						1
2	3	4	5	6	7	8
9	10	11 Veterans' Day	12	13	14	15
16	17	18	19	20	21	22
23	24	25	26	27 Thanksgiving	28	29
30						

Notes

"Never trust a man who hates cats."
— JANE PAULEY

December 2025

SUNDAY	MONDAY	TUESDAY	WEDNESDAY	THURSDAY	FRIDAY	SATURDAY
	1	2	3	4	5	6
7	8	9	10	11	12	13
14 Hanakkah	15	16	17	18	19	20
21	22	23	24	25 Christmas Day	26 Kwanzaa	27
28	29	30	31			

Notes

"Dogs believe they are human. Cats believe they are God."
— ANONYMOUS

January 2026

SUNDAY	MONDAY	TUESDAY	WEDNESDAY	THURSDAY	FRIDAY	SATURDAY
				1 New Year's Day	2	3
4	5	6	7	8	9	10
11	12	13	14	15	16	17
18	19 Martin Luther King Day	20	21	22	23	24
25	26	27	28	29	30	31

Notes

"Cats are connoisseurs of comfort."
— JAMES HERRIOT

February 2026

SUNDAY	MONDAY	TUESDAY	WEDNESDAY	THURSDAY	FRIDAY	SATURDAY
1	2	3	4	5	6	7
8	9	10	11	12	13	14 Valentine's Day
15	16 Presidents Day	17	18	19	20	21
22	23	24	25	26	27	28

Notes

"Time spent with cats is never wasted."
— SIGMUND FREUD

March 2026

SUNDAY	MONDAY	TUESDAY	WEDNESDAY	THURSDAY	FRIDAY	SATURDAY
1	2	3	4	5	6	7
8	9	10	11	12	13	14
15	16	17	18	19	20	21
22	23	24	25	26	27	28
29	30	31				

Notes

"If animals could speak, the dog would be a blundering outspoken fellow; but the cat would have the rare grace of never saying a word too much."
— MARK TWAIN

April 2026

SUNDAY	MONDAY	TUESDAY	WEDNESDAY	THURSDAY	FRIDAY	SATURDAY
			1	2	3	4
5 Easter	6	7	8	9	10	11
12	13	14	15	16	17	18
19	20	21	22	23	24	25
26	27	28	29	30		

Notes

"I wish that my writing was as mysterious as a cat."
— EDGAR ALLAN POE

May 2026

SUNDAY	MONDAY	TUESDAY	WEDNESDAY	THURSDAY	FRIDAY	SATURDAY
					1	2
3	4	5	6	7	8	9
10 Mother's Day	11	12	13	14	15	16
17	18	19	20	21	22	23
24	25 Memorial Day	26	27	28	29	30
31						

Notes

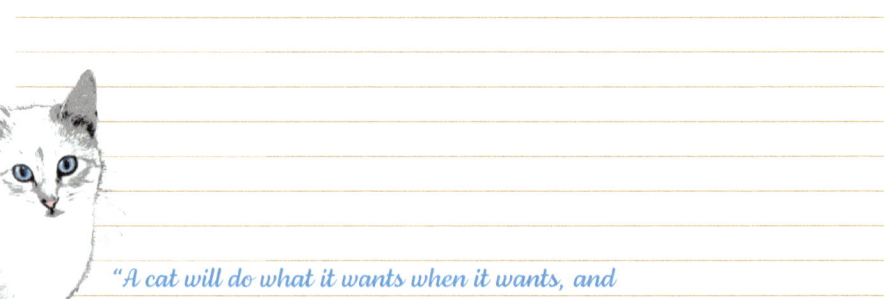

"A cat will do what it wants when it wants, and there's not a thing you can do about it."
— FRANK PERKINS

June 2026

SUNDAY	MONDAY	TUESDAY	WEDNESDAY	THURSDAY	FRIDAY	SATURDAY
	1	2	3	4	5	6
7	8	9	10	11	12	13
14	15	16	17	18	19 Juneteenth	20
21 Father's Day	22	23	24	25	26	27
28	29	30				

Notes

"The only thing a cat worries about is what's happening right now."
— LLOYD ALEXANDER

July 2026

SUNDAY	MONDAY	TUESDAY	WEDNESDAY	THURSDAY	FRIDAY	SATURDAY
			1	2	3	4 Independence Day
5	6	7	8	9	10	11
12	13	14	15	16	17	18
19	20	21	22	23	24	25
26	27	28	29	30	31	

Notes

> *"Dogs come when they're called.
> Cats take a message and get
> back to you later."*
> — MARY BLY

August 2026

SUNDAY	MONDAY	TUESDAY	WEDNESDAY	THURSDAY	FRIDAY	SATURDAY
						1
2	3	4	5	6	7	8
9	10	11	12	13	14	15
16	17	18	19	20	21	22
23	24	25	26	27	28	29
30	31					

Notes

"To err is human, to purr is feline."
— ROBERT BYRNE

September 2026

SUNDAY	MONDAY	TUESDAY	WEDNESDAY	THURSDAY	FRIDAY	SATURDAY
		1	2	3	4	5
6	7 Labor Day	8	9	10	11	12
13	14	15	16	17	18	19
20	21	22	23	24	25	26
27	28	29	30			

Notes

"Dogs eat. Cats dine."
— ANN TAYLOR

October 2026

SUNDAY	MONDAY	TUESDAY	WEDNESDAY	THURSDAY	FRIDAY	SATURDAY
				1	2	3
4	5	6	7	8	9	10
11	12 Columbus Day	13	14	15	16	17
18	19	20	21	22	23	24
25	26	27	28	29	30	31 Halloween

Notes

"No cat purrs unless someone is around to listen."
— ELIZABETH MARSHALL THOMAS

November 2026

SUNDAY	MONDAY	TUESDAY	WEDNESDAY	THURSDAY	FRIDAY	SATURDAY
1	2	3	4	5	6	7
8	9	10	11 Veterans' Day	12	13	14
15	16	17	18	19	20	21
22	23	24	25	26 Thanksgiving	27	28
29	30					

Notes

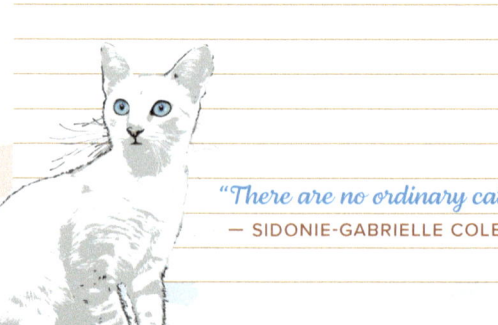

"There are no ordinary cats."
— SIDONIE-GABRIELLE COLETTE

December 2026

SUNDAY	MONDAY	TUESDAY	WEDNESDAY	THURSDAY	FRIDAY	SATURDAY
		1	2	3	4　Hanukkah	5
6	7	8	9	10	11	12
13	14	15	16	17	18	19
20	21	22	23	24	25　Christmas Day	26　Kwanzaa
27	28	29	30	31		

Notes

"A cat doesn't care if you are smart or dumb, give him your heart and he will give you his."
— ABRAHAM LINCOLN

Notes

"Sip slow. Purr more."
— SNOWBABY, THE CAT

OTHER TITLES BY
Annette Bridges

BOOKS:

When Cattitude Meets Coffee Playful quotes for coffee lovers.

Mamma Said So 20 Pearls of Wisdom from a Southern Sage.

101 Things Women Want from Their Men Written collectively by hundreds of women who shared their advice.

A Dachshund Tale Lessons learned from my dog.

Oh, How the Years Fly By! A whimsical inspirational quote book.

The Gospel According to Mamma One mother's philosophy on love, God, money, aging, decisions, change, and much more.

Be Queen of Your Life A savvy mom helps daughters command and rule their lives.

Have Lipstick, Will Travel How to reimagine your life, purpose, and hair color.

COLORING BOOKS:

Color-N-Doodle Your World An inspiring collection of coloring pages with your own space to doodle and create.

Oh, How the Years Fly By! A whimsical adult coloring book.

JOURNALS:

Okay, We Grew Old Together… Now What? A couple's journal.

My Furry Friend A keepsake journal.

Anytime Journal Because anytime is a good time to journal.

Jot Journals 18 themed pocket-sized journals.

Color Your World Journal Series 18 themed large journals.

BOOKS FOR CHILDREN:

Lady and Bella: Totally Different, Totally Friends A coloring storybook for children.

Lady and Bella: Totally Friends Journal Especially for children.

Lady and Bella's Alphabet Kitchen A to Z recipes for kid cooks.

www.ingramcontent.com/pod-product-compliance
Lightning Source LLC
Chambersburg PA
CBHW041725070526
44586CB00001B/5